W9-BFB-180

Lobster

Elaine Elliot and Virginia Lee

Formac Publishing Company Limited
Halifax, Nova Scotia

Authors' note

In continuing the theme of the **Flavours** *series of cookbooks, we invited chefs from across Canada to share their recipes. Each recipe has been tested and adjusted for the home cook.*

— Elaine Elliot and Virginia Lee

Participating restaurants

British Columbia
All Seasons Café, Nelson
C Restaurant, Vancouver
Diva at the Met, Vancouver
Le Gavroche, Vancouver
Old House Restaurant, Courtenay
Raincity Grill, Vancouver
Alberta
Catch Restaurant, Calgary
Lake Louise Station, Lake Louise
Saskatchewan
Boffins Club, Saskatoon
Manitoba
Step'n Out Eclectic Cuisine, Winnipeg
Ontario
Edgewater Manor Restaurant, Stoney Creek
Little Inn of Bayfield, Bayfield
Vineland Estates Winery Restaurant, Vineland
Québec
Maestro SVP, Montreal
New Brunswick
Compass Rose, Grand Manan Island
Dufferin Inn and San Martello Dining Room, Saint John

Inn on the Cove and Spa, Saint John
Marshlands Inn, Sackville
Quaco Inn, St. Martins
Prince Edward Island
Dalvay by the Sea, Dalvay
The Dunes Café, Brackley Beach
Off-Broadway Café, Charlottetown
Shaw's Hotel, Brackley Beach
The Inn at Bay Fortune, Bay Fortune
Nova Scotia
Acton's Grill and Café, Wolfville
Amherst Shore Country Inn, Lorneville
Blomidon Inn, Wolfville
Da Maurizio, Halifax
Duncreigan Country Inn, Mabou
Haddon Hall Inn, Chester
Inn on the Lake, Fall River
Innlet Café, Mahone Bay
La Perla, Dartmouth
Mountain Gap Inn, Smiths Cove
Nemo's Restaurant, Halifax
Stories Restaurant at Halliburton House Inn, Halifax

Copyright © 2005 Formac Publishing Company
All rights reserved. No part of this book may be reproduced or transmitted in any form or by any means, electronic or mechanical, including photocopying, or by any information storage or retrieval system, without permission in writing from the publisher.
Formac Publishing Company Limited acknowledges the support of the Culture Division, Nova Scotia Department of Tourism, Culture and Heritage. We acknowledge the financial support of the Government of Canada through the Book Publishing Industry Development Program (BPIDP) for our publishing activities.
We acknowledge the support of the Canada Council for the Arts for our publishing program.

Library and Archives Canada Cataloguing in Publication
Elliot, Elaine, 1939-
        Lobster : recipes from Canadian chefs coast to coast / Elaine
Elliot & Virginia Lee. (Flavours series)
Includes index.
ISBN 10: 0-88780-679-1, ISBN 13: 978-0-88780-679-7
        1. Cookery (Lobsters) 2. Cookery (Shellfish) I. Lee, Virginia,
1947- II. Title. III. Series.
TX754.L63E45 2005   641.6'95   C2005-903634-6

Formac Publishing Company Limited
5502 Atlantic Street
Halifax, Nova Scotia B3H 1G4
www.formac.ca

Printed and bound in China

Contents

Introduction   5

Starters   15

Soups   31

Luncheon   45

Main Courses   67

Index   94

Photo Credits   96

Introduction

It's hard to believe that lobster hasn't always been regarded as the gourmet food it is today. Just a few decades ago, for many fishermen's families in Atlantic Canada, eating lobster was a sign of poverty—it meant that you were too poor to buy bologna. Now, thanks to gourmet styles and a strong interest in seafood, lobster appears on menus across the country and is served at community-run lobster suppers throughout the Maritime provinces. This book of recipes from chefs across Canada demonstrates how versatile lobster and other popular shellfish can be in appetizers, soups, lunches and entrées.

Lobsters (*Homarus americanus*) are caught from the ocean floor. Studies have shown that early juveniles prefer rocky, cobbled bottoms, while adults are generally regarded as relatively solitary, highly migratory animals. A lobster grows by moulting, or shedding, its shell; this occurs about 25 times during the first five years of life, increasing the lobster's size 20 per cent each time. After a moult, which usually takes place in the summer, the lobster is soft-shelled and filled with the seawater it has absorbed in the process.

Up to two months passes before the water is replaced by new lobster flesh. As the shell hardens in the cold waters of the North Atlantic, the lobster acquires a denser, fuller feel, giving the meat the texture and taste that consumers prefer. It takes five years for a lobster to grow to one pound and up to 20 years for it to reach four pounds.

⚓

Lobsters are most abundant off the coasts of Nova Scotia, New Brunswick and Prince Edward Island, and in the Gulf of St. Lawrence and the Gulf of Maine. They're harvested and processed in the three Maritime provinces, Newfoundland and Quebec. Landings peak twice a year, once from April to June, when the spring season opens, and again in December, after the winter fishery starts in southwestern Nova Scotia.

Atlantic Canada's staggered fishing seasons are designed to protect the stock, and the waters are divided into 41 lobster fishing areas, each with its own season varying in length from eight weeks to eight months. This seasonal effort is comple- mented by new and innovative holding and processing techniques. Most of the lobster fishery takes place fairly close to shore, but a few vessels fish the deep basins and outer banks off southwestern Nova Scotia. Five provinces participate in the catch, with Nova Scotia, New Brunswick and Prince Edward Island accounting for 90 per cent of lobster landings and Quebec and Newfoundland making up the remaining 10 per cent. Currently, there are about 9,000 licensed lobster fishermen, of which nearly 3,000 are in Nova Scotia.

Licensed lobster fishermen—usually a captain and two or three crew members—set their traps from small boats, heading out on the water in the early hours of the morning and staying out for up to 12 hours. The brightly coloured buoys mark the areas where they leave their traps. They return several hours later to haul up the wooden-frame or plastic-coated steel-mesh traps from the sea floor.

In Prince Edward Island, lobster has been the mainstay of the economy since the fishery began in the mid-1870s, although it almost died in its infancy. In the mid-1880s—only 10 years after the boom began—over-fishing drove the stocks to dangerously low levels, and the fishery faced ruin. It was saved by a combination of regulation, co-operation and luck.

Commercial canning helped the lobster fishery flourish in all parts of the Maritimes. The first known cannery opened on Prince Edward Island in 1858. Within 25 years, thanks to the lobster fishery, the number of Island canneries had risen to more than 100, and the lobster fishery accounted for 25 per cent of the province's income. Without canning, the lobster would never have found its way to lucrative markets in Great Britain and the United States, where it was considered a delicacy.

The success and prosperity of the present-day lobster fishery is evident in towns and villages across the Maritimes. It challenges the stereotype of hardscrabble life in a fishing village. Inevitably there has been controversy about the control of licenses, fishing seasons and the number of traps

in a given area. In 1999, the New Brunswick community of Burnt Church became a hotbed of tension between native and non-native lobster fishermen. The native fishermen were exercising their treaty right to set lobster traps throughout the year, regardless of the season. During the often violent demonstrations, non-native fishermen destroyed native traps, fish plants, boats and equipment.

A moratorium helped defuse the trouble, and in 2002, the federal government released a report aimed at preventing more conflict. It recommended that all charges stemming from the confrontation be dropped and that Ottawa should compensate the fishermen for their lost traps and boats. It also recommended that native fishermen adhere to the same season as non-natives, meaning they would be banned from fishing lobster in the fall.

⚓

Traditionally, live lobsters are held in pounds—large, fenced areas of the ocean—but recently, huge dry-land holding facilities pioneered in Atlantic Canada have made possible a three-million-pound live inventory of the region's best lobsters. As a result, international buyers can get a year-round supply of the top-quality Canadian crustaceans. Lobster is Canada's most valuable seafood export, contributing as much as $1 billion in export sales each year.

Larger lobsters generally are sold in the fresh, live market where they command top prices, while smaller ones are cooked and either frozen whole or shelled for meat. Most of the lobsters caught in the waters of Nova Scotia, Newfoundland and Quebec go to the live market, which means consumers can select and buy them from tanks in grocery stores, fish markets or directly from fishermen at the wharf.

Clearwater Seafoods, a Nova Scotia company, has become almost synonymous with lobster. In 1976, it started out as a small, local distributor, with two co-owners running the business out of a pickup truck. They quickly developed a strategy and infrastructure for storing lobsters and distributing to markets worldwide. From their company headquarters in Bedford they started shipping planeloads of live lobster to destinations in Europe and the United States. The company has joined forces with the government to ensure the responsible management of lobster stocks. It is also dedicated to putting new and improved technology in place.

In Arichat, Cape Breton, one million lobsters can be found resting in "private apartments," where temperatures are maintained just above the freezing mark. This hi-tech Clearwater facility is designed to store lobsters for long periods of time. Tricked into thinking it's always winter, they don't moult when summer arrives and continue to grow and mature in the safety of their compartment. Sixty people work in the plant, sometimes around the clock. At times, the volume of lobsters arriving in a single day can reach 100,000.

⚓

Sold live, cooked, frozen and canned to consumers in more than 55 countries around the

world, lobster is one of the exports most closely associated with Canada. Almost every part of a lobster can be used in some culinary way, except for the digestive tract, the antennae and mouth parts. The empty shells can be used in bisques or for lobster au gratin; the green tomalley that fills the cooked body cavity is excellent in spreads, sauces, dips and butters; and the roe—the red unfertilized eggs—is also very tasty.

Served hot, lobster meat adds richness to casseroles, stir-fries, stuffings, sauces, bisques, omelettes, soufflés, quiches and many other dishes. Cold, it's wonderful in salads, hors d'oeuvres and the famous East Coast lobster roll. The recipes in this book range from Lobster and Potato Salad to Huron County Lobster Chowder, to Barbecued Lobster with Red Pepper and Lime Butter.

Lobster meat is an excellent source of protein, more healthful than hamburger and nearly fat-free—as long as it's not dipped in drawn butter. It contains many minerals and vitamins, as well as omega-3 fatty acids, which help reduce the risk of heart attack.

Traditional lobster suppers are perhaps most popular throughout Prince Edward Island, although they also are held in many other Atlantic Canadian communities. At these suppers, which are generally held from early June to mid-October, a succulent whole, cooked lobster is served in its shell, often with a sidedish of seafood chowder, a freshly baked roll, salad and a dessert, such as blueberry pie. Diners indulge in the ritual art of extracting cooked lobster from the shell. This takes some practice and is messy enough to require a bib and several napkins. After a few attempts, one gets the hang of using a lobster cracker and a pick to pry and pull out the meat. And after the first taste, most aficionados never let a summer go by without one communal lobster supper.

⚓

This book also includes recipes for other favourite Canadian shellfish, including the various species of crab. On the East Coast, the most popular is the Atlantic snow crab (*Chionoecetes opilio*), which is occasionally called spider crab or queen crab. Only the males are harvested because females never exceed the legal minimum size. As with the lobster fishery, the government carefully regulates the number of licenses and fishing seasons. Atlantic snow crab and rock crab (*Cancer irrovatus*) are harvested in the Gulf of St. Lawrence and off Cape Breton Island and Newfoundland, forming a lucrative fishing-and-processing industry.

Most common to the Pacific West Coast is the Dungeness crab (*Cancer magister*) and the King crab (Paralithodes camtschatica), the patriarch of the crab family, which is sometimes called the Alaska king crab. Dungeness crabs are found from Alaska to California, and this fishery has an important economic impact on Vancouver Island and its surrounding areas. Crabs are marketed whole, live or cooked. Alternatively, crab meat is sold in cans or frozen packages.

Mussels, clams and scallops are small edible shellfish found in most fish markets. Aquaculture

of mussels has been a high-growth industry in the Atlantic region, particularly in Prince Edward Island. Today the province produces more than 80 per cent of the mussel landings in Canada, contributes about $50 million to the provincial economy and employs about 1,500 Islanders.

These bivalves grow on long lines suspended in the water and are harvested in winter and spring when the flesh is in its best form. They're sold live, and the shells can be lightly tapped before cooking to make sure that the mussel closes tightly, indicating that it is alive. It is recommended never to cook and eat any that are not alive, and to discard any that gape open or have broken shells.

Clams, like mussels, are sold live in the shell, or uncooked and shucked in plastic containers. Processed clams are also readily available in cans. The Nova Scotia soft-shell clam (*Mya aremaria*) and the hard-shell quahog (*Mercenaria mercenaria*) are the most prized. On the West Coast, the manila clam (*Tapes pilippinarum*) and the littleneck clam (*Protoaca staminea*) are most frequently harvested in the wild or farmed.

One of the most succulent shellfish species is the sea scallop (*Placopecten magellanicus*), which is found along the eastern North Atlantic, from the northern Gulf of St. Lawrence to northern Newfoundland and Cape Hatteras, North Carolina. The ivory to pinkish-white meat is the adductor muscle that holds the shell together. Since scallops survive for only a short time out of the water, they must be shucked after harvesting and sold fresh or frozen. The term "scallop" shouldn't be confused with the American bay scallop (*Argopecten irradians*), which also is found in Atlantic waters, but is much smaller.

Pacific Coast scallops include spiny scallops (*Chlamys hastate*) and pink scallops (*Chlamys rubida*). Found mainly on the west coast of Vancouver Island and in the Strait of Georgia, these smaller species range in colour from ivory to pinkish-white or pale golden brown. Their texture is similar to sea scallops and their flavour is both sweet and briny. Most scallops are harvested in the wild; however, scientists on both coasts are studying how to farm them through aquaculture.

There are many shrimp species on the market today, and they come in several different sizes and from numerous sources. They are harvested wild and also raised in shrimp farms. Shrimp, also known as prawns, are available fresh, frozen, cooked and raw, as well as shelled, unshelled and canned. They range in size from a tiny salad shrimp to jumbo shrimp and take very little time to cook.

The recipes in this revised edition of *Lobster*, which have been provided by talented chefs from across Canada, are for a wide range of rich and mouthwatering crab, lobster, clam, mussel, shrimp and scallop dishes. Thanks to innovations in delivering fresh shellfish, freezing and canning, they can be prepared throughout the year. While lobster remains the biggest crowd pleaser, all of the dishes featured in this book celebrate the gourmet rewards of the sea.

*Fresh lobster meat can be used to create delicious starters such as
Lobster-stuffed Mushroom Caps, p.19.*

Starters

In our travels we have found talented chefs utilizing the ocean's bounty in a variety of first-course dishes. From crab cakes to steamed clams, we are sure that you will want to try these creations.

Hot Atlantic Crab Dip

Easily prepared in advance, this dish has become a favourite at social gatherings. It will disappear quickly from your buffet table when your friends arrive!

12 oz (375 g) Atlantic crab meat
8 oz (250 g) cream cheese, softened
4 tbsp (60 mL) egg-based mayonnaise
salt and pepper to taste
assorted crackers

Pick over crab to remove any shell or cartilage. Blend crab, cream cheese and mayonnaise; season with salt and pepper. Turn into a shallow baking dish; cover and refrigerate. At serving time, preheat oven to 325°F (160°C) and bake for 30 minutes or until browned on top and bubbly. Serve with assorted crackers.

Yields 2 cups.

Cozze al Forno
(Broiled Mussels)

La Perla, Dartmouth, NS

At La Perla, these mussels are drizzled with additional garlic butter. For an elegant presentation, serve them nestled on a platter of rock salt.

12 oz (360 g) fresh spinach, washed and
  stemmed
2 lb (1 kg) fresh mussels, scrubbed and
  debearded
2 tbsp (30 mL) garlic butter
½ cup (125 mL) onion, finely chopped
½ cup (125 mL) ricotta cheese
salt and pepper to taste
3 oz (100 g) provolone cheese, grated

Blanch spinach for 30 seconds. Cool, squeeze out excess moisture and chop. Reserve.

Steam prepared mussels in ¼ cup (60 mL) water until shells open, about 5 minutes. Discard any that do not open. Refresh in cold water and remove half the shell so you are left with a mussel on the half-shell.

Preheat oven broiler. In a medium-sized skillet, melt garlic butter and sauté onion until translucent. Add spinach and cook for 2 minutes. Stir in ricotta, salt and pepper. Remove from heat, cool and add provolone. Arrange mussels on a large baking tray. Top mussels with spinach mixture and place under broiler until hot. Drizzle with additional melted garlic butter, if desired.

Serves 4.

Lobster-stuffed Mushroom Caps

Off-Broadway Café, Charlottetown, PEI

Peter Williams of the Off-Broadway Café serves mushroom caps stuffed with lobster, drizzled with a rich béarnaise sauce and topped with grated Jarlsberg cheese. We suggest making this decadent appetizer for a special occasion.

16 large mushroom caps, stems removed
4 tbsp (60 mL) butter, portioned
2 tbsp (30 mL) all-purpose flour
½ cup (125 mL) heavy cream (35% M.F.)
1 tbsp (15 mL) dry white vermouth
2 tbsp (30 mL) lobster or fish broth
scant pinch of nutmeg
pinch of cayenne pepper
1 tsp (5 mL) paprika
8 oz (225 g) fresh lobster meat, in small pieces
béarnaise sauce (recipe follows)
½ cup (125 mL) grated Jarlsberg cheese

Clean mushroom caps. Melt 2 tablespoons (30 mL) butter in a skillet over medium heat and sauté mushrooms until slightly browned and tender. Place mushrooms in a single layer in the bottom of a shallow baking dish. Set aside.

Melt remaining amount of butter in a large saucepan. Whisk in flour and cook until roux is bubbly and slightly browned, about 5 minutes. Stir in cream, vermouth and broth; cook, stirring constantly, until thickened. Season with nutmeg, pepper and paprika. Fold in lobster meat and spoon into mushroom caps. Top each mushroom with a tablespoon of Béarnaise Sauce, sprinkle with grated cheese and broil, 6 inches from the element, until hot and bubbly.

Serves 4-6.

Béarnaise Sauce

3 egg yolks
1 tsp (5 mL) lemon juice
1½ tsp (7 mL) cider vinegar
½ tsp (2 mL) dried tarragon
½ cup (125 mL) unsalted butter, melted

In a food processor, blend egg yolks, lemon juice, vinegar and tarragon for 10 seconds. Continue to process while slowly adding melted butter in a steady stream. Serve immediately.

Dungeness Crab-stuffed Heirloom Tomatoes

Raincity Grill, Vancouver, BC

Heirloom tomatoes are not new; in fact, as their name implies, they are traditional fruits, which have been grown from seeds untouched by human intervention. Heirlooms come in a variety of colours and shapes, and are noted for their flavour.

4 heirloom tomatoes
6 oz (185 g) Dungeness crab meat
1 shallot, finely minced
2 cloves garlic, minced
2 tbsp (30 mL) finely chopped basil leaves
¼ cup (50 mL) butter, softened salt and pepper
trio of pepper sauce (recipe follows)

Using a sharp knife, remove a sliver off the bottom of each tomato so they will stand in a baking dish. Take a ¼-inch (0.5-cm) slice off the top of each tomato and scoop out the seeds with a teaspoon, being careful to keep the tomatoes' shape.

Preheat oven to 325°F (160°C). Carefully pick over crab meat, removing any shell or cartilage. Combine crab, shallot, garlic, basil and butter; season with salt and pepper. Gently stuff tomato shells and cover with tomato top. Bake for 10-15 minutes, until heated through. Reserve and keep warm.

Trio of Pepper Sauce

1 each yellow, red and orange sweet pepper
3 tbsp (45 mL) grape seed oil (or olive oil)
salt and pepper

Toss the peppers in a bowl with oil, then roast in a 400°F (200°C) oven for 20 minutes. Place the peppers back in the bowl, cover with plastic wrap, and let rest until cool. Peel peppers; halve and remove seeds. Using a blender, purée each pepper separately until smooth. Season with salt and pepper to taste.

To serve: drizzle a little of each pepper sauce on plate and top with a warm stuffed tomato.

Serves 4.

Cream Cheese Crab Cakes

Boffins Club, Saskatoon, SK

The sweet crab flavour and creamy cheese centre of these cakes make a delicious first course. For a luncheon dish or main-course entrée, just add a salad and warm crusty bread.

¼ cup (60 mL) finely chopped red bell pepper
¼ cup (60 mL) finely sliced green onion
¼ cup (60 mL) finely sliced celery
1 tbsp (15 mL) fresh lemon juice
1 tbsp (15 mL) jalapeño hot sauce, or to taste
8 oz (250 g) whipped cream cheese, room
    temperature
1 cup (250 mL) fine bread crumbs
½ tsp (2 mL) thyme
½ tsp (2 mL) basil
pinch of salt
pinch of pepper
1 lb (450 g) lump crabmeat
2 -3 tbsp (30-45 mL) butter
creole mustard sauce (recipe follows)
fresh herbs

In a skillet over medium heat, sauté pepper, onion, celery, lemon juice and pepper sauce until the vegetables wilt, about 5 minutes. Remove from heat and stir in whipped cream cheese until combined. Set aside. In a bowl, combine bread crumbs, thyme, basil, salt and pepper. Set aside.

Clean and check crab for shell and cartilage; squeeze gently to remove excess liquid. Cup your hand and place about 2 tbsp (30 mL) of the crabmeat into it. With a blunt knife, spread about 2 tbsp (30 mL) of the cream cheese mixture over the crabmeat. Add another 2 tbsp (30 mL) of the crabmeat, press down and form into a ball. Roll the ball in the crumb mixture until well coated. Place ball on a cutting board and press lightly to form a cake about ¾ inch (2 cm) thick. Repeat process to form 12 crabcakes.

Heat butter in a skillet over medium heat. Add crab cakes, being careful not to crowd, and sauté until golden on both sides.

To serve: arrange 2 or 3 cakes on each serving plate, drizzle with Creole Mustard Sauce and garnish with fresh herbs.

Serves 4-6.

Creole Mustard Sauce

3 tbsp (45 mL) pepper jelly
¼ cup (60 mL) fresh orange juice
¼ cup (60 mL) Creole mustard

In a small saucepan over low heat, combine
pepper jelly, orange juice and mustard; stir until
sauce consistency. Serve warm.

Yields ½ cup.

Simply Steamed Clams

C Restaurant, Vancouver, BC

Executive Chef Robert Clark may imply that this dish is simple—and indeed it is simple to prepare—but the flavour is anything but ordinary. Be sure to have plenty of warm crusty bread on hand for dipping in the buttery herb sauce.

4 lb (2 kg) clams in the shell
6 tbsp (90 mL) butter, portioned
⅓ cup (75 mL) chopped shallots
⅔ cup (150 mL) white wine
1 cup (250 mL) cherry or grape tomatoes, cut
  in quarters
2 tbsp (30 mL) chopped fresh herbs of choice
  (suggestions: chervil, cilantro, parsley,
  tarragon)

Wash clams. In a heavy sauté pan over medium-high heat, heat 2 tbsp (30 mL) butter. Add clams; cover and steam for 2 minutes. Lower heat to medium, add shallots and sweat for about 2 minutes. Raise heat slightly, add wine and cook until clams open, about 2-4 minutes. Add remaining butter, tomatoes and herbs; toss together until butter is melted and tomatoes are slightly wilted.

To serve: discard any clams that did not open. Divide clams with sauce into 4 large bowls and serve with fresh hot bread.

Serves 4.

Roasted Roma Tomatoes with Scallops

Lake Louise Station, Lake Louise, AB

At Lake Louise Station, Chef Hung Khuu finishes off his scallop dish with balsamic vinegar. He serves it as an appetizer on a bed of mixed lettuce or mesclun, but by increasing the portions it may be served as an entrée on pasta topped with Parmesan, butter and a drizzle of the cooking sauce.

¾ lb (375 g) sea scallops
6 small Roma tomatoes
½ cup (125 mL) extra virgin olive oil
2 shallots, diced
1 large clove garlic, minced
3 tbsp (45 mL) fresh basil leaves, finely chopped
salt and freshly ground pepper
¼ cup (60 mL) sliced black (kalamata) olives
½ cup (125 mL) good-quality balsamic vinegar
mesclun salad greens to serve 4
fresh basil leaves, as garnish

Rinse scallops and pat dry. Slice tomatoes in half and scoop out seeds and membrane with a teaspoon. If necessary, take a small sliver off the bottom so that the tomatoes will balance on a plate. Invert onto paper towels and set aside.

Heat olive oil in a skillet over medium heat and sauté shallots, garlic and scallops until scallops are partially cooked, about 3 minutes. Season with salt and pepper. Remove scallops and set aside. Add balsamic vinegar to pan and remove from heat.

Preheat oven to 375°F (190°C). Place tomato halves in a shallow baking dish; add a small amount of oil mixture to each tomato and stuff with a scallop. Top with remaining oil. Divide sliced olives among scallops and bake for 10 minutes. Serve on a bed of mesclun salad greens, garnished with fresh basil leaves.

Serves 4.

Shellfish with Yucatan Flavours

Old House Restaurant, Courtenay, BC

Laced with spices and natural citrus flavours, this mouthwatering shellfish dish will have you yearning for an exotic southern vacation. This recipe lends itself to preparation in advance; simply assemble and pop in the oven.

4 lb shellfish of choice (e.g. 2 kg mussels, clams, shrimp)
3 garlic cloves, minced
1 jalapeño pepper, seeded and chopped
1 tbsp (15 mL) chili powder
1 tbsp (15 mL) paprika
1 tsp (5 mL) ground cumin
½ tsp (2 mL) oregano
¼ tsp (1 mL) ground cinnamon
¼ tsp (1 mL) ground cloves
2 tbsp (30 mL) beer
juice of 1 lime and 1 orange
2 tbsp (30 mL) olive oil
2 tbsp (30 mL) chopped cilantro
fresh cilantro and orange wedges, as garnish

Rinse shellfish with fresh cold water and drain. Discard any clams or mussels that are cracked or do not close when lightly tapped. Set aside in a large bowl.

Preheat oven to 425°F (220°C). In a blender, combine garlic, jalapeño pepper, dry spices, beer, lime and orange juices and olive oil; purée until smooth. Pour marinade over shellfish, toss to coat and let stand for 5 minutes.

Pour shellfish and marinade into a large shallow roasting pan. Bake, uncovered, stirring once after 10 minutes. Continue baking until mussels and clams have fully opened, about 5-10 minutes longer. Discard any shellfish that did not open.

To serve: Pour onto one large or 6 individual serving dishes; garnish with chopped cilantro and accompany with orange wedges.

Serves 6.

Dungeness Crab Salad

Le Gavroche, Vancouver, BC

Sweet, fresh Pacific Dungeness crab blends well with the fresh lime and cilantro flavours of this interesting salad. Manuel Ferreira of Le Gavroche presents the crab on crisp green asparagus, but feel free to serve with other green salads.

12 green asparagus spears
1 lb (450 g) fresh Dungeness crab meat
4-5 tbsp (60-75 mL) fresh lime juice
2 tbsp (30 mL) extra virgin olive oil
1 tsp (5 mL) crushed pink peppercorns
¼ cup (60 mL) chopped fresh cilantro
1 large avocado, peeled and cubed
salt
cilantro sprigs and lime wedges, as garnish

Trim asparagus and steam until *al dente*. Drain and rinse under cold water to stop cooking; set aside. Clean and check crab meat for shell and cartilage; squeeze gently to remove excess liquid and set aside.

In a bowl, combine lime juice, olive oil, peppercorns and cilantro; add crab meat and avocado and stir to combine. Adjust seasoning with salt to taste and marinate for 30 minutes.

To serve: fan three asparagus spears on each of 4 serving plates; place a spoonful of crab mixture where the stalks meet. Garnish with lime wedges and a sprig of cilantro.

Serves 4.

Lobster Potato Salad

Catch Restaurant, Calgary, AB

At Catch Restaurant, the chef serves this delectable salad garnished with oven-dried strawberries.

2 whole lobsters (1 lb/500 g each)
8 large strawberries, quartered
¼ cup (60 mL) balsamic vinegar
1 lb (500 g) fingerling or baby potatoes, halved
1 shallot, sliced
1 clove garlic, crushed
2 sprigs fresh thyme
½ tsp (2 mL) salt
1 bay leaf
½ tsp (2 mL) crushed black pepper
olive oil
½ cup (125 mL) mayonnaise
1 tbsp (15 mL) grainy mustard
½ lemon, juiced
chopped chives, as garnish

Cook lobsters in boiling salted water for 10 minutes. Drain and rinse under cold running water. Remove lobster from shell, being careful to keep claws intact. Chop lobster tail meat into 1-inch (3-cm) pieces and refrigerate.

Preheat oven to 250°F (120°C). Toss strawberry quarters with balsamic vinegar and spread on a baking sheet. Bake until dried and slightly wrinkled, about 40 minutes. Cool and reserve.

Place potatoes, shallot, garlic, thyme, bay leaf, salt and pepper in a saucepan and add enough olive oil to cover potatoes. Bring to a slow simmer and cook until potatoes are tender. Cool potatoes in the oil, then drain. Remove bay leaf and thyme sprigs.

While potatoes are cooling, combine mayonnaise, mustard and lemon juice. To serve, toss potatoes with mayonnaise and reserved lobster meat. Divide among four plates and top each salad with a lobster claw. Garnish with strawberries and chopped chives.

Serves 4.

Mediterranean Seafood Stew, p.37

Soups

You can never have too many soups or chowders in your recipe collection, and we are sure you will be intrigued by these unique ones. Wow your guests with spicy Thai Crab Noodle Soup, the creation of the chef at All Seasons Café in Nelson, BC, or serve a crowd the hearty Mediterranean Seafood Stew, a delight from Nemo's Restaurant in Halifax, NS.

Dunes' Seafood Chowder with Lobster

The Dunes Café, Brackley Beach, PEI

The chef at the Dunes Café prepares his fish stock in advance. While we offer his directions for stock, novice cooks can substitute bottled clam juice or stock made from powdered fish bouillon.

4 cups (1 L) fish stock (recipe follows)
4 tbsp (60 mL) butter
4 tbsp (60 mL) all-purpose flour
⅛ tsp (0.5 mL) nutmeg
salt and white pepper to taste
4 large potatoes, peeled and cut in large dice
4 tbsp (60 mL) butter (2nd amount)
½ cup (125 g) chopped onion
½ cup (125 g) chopped celery
1 lb (500 g) lobster meat
3 oz (100 g) salmon fillet, in small chunks
3 oz (100 g) sole or haddock fillets, in small chunks
4 oz (125 g) shrimp, shelled
½ lb (225 g) mussels, steamed and shelled
1 cup (250 mL) heavy cream (35% M.F.)

Place fish stock in a large pot and heat to a simmer. Combine butter and flour to make a paste. Whisk butter mixture into hot stock, bring to a boil and cook 2 minutes, stirring constantly. Season with nutmeg, salt and pepper; set aside.

Cook potato cubes gently in salted water until just tender. Drain and reserve.

Melt second amount of butter in a skillet and sauté onion and celery until soft. Stir in all of the seafood and simmer 3 minutes. Combine seafood and reserved potatoes with thickened fish stock and adjust seasonings, if necessary. Add cream and bring to serving temperature. Do not boil.

Serves 4-6.

Fish Stock
6 cups (1.5 L) water
1 lb (450 g) fish bones
1 bay leaf
3 whole cloves
1 medium onion, peeled

Place water and fish bones in a large kettle. Stick bay leaf and cloves into onion and add to pot. Bring to a boil, reduce heat and simmer 20 minutes. Strain.

Gazpacho with Shrimp

Haddon Hall Inn, Chester, NS

The chef at Haddon Hall Inn adds a touch of the Mediterranean to his summer menu during the hot sunny days of August! Remember, the soup is prepared early and chilled for about 12 hours to allow the flavours to blend.

1 medium onion
1 garlic clove
½ English cucumber, pared and seeded
1 green pepper, in chunks
4-5 large vine-ripened tomatoes
½ cup (125 mL) oil
¼ cup (60 mL) vinegar
2 cups (500 mL) water
½ tbsp (8 mL) paprika
1 slice of bread
pinch of caraway seeds
4 whole peppercorns
salt
4 oz (125 g) fresh shrimp

Combine all ingredients except shrimp and process in batches in a food processor or blender. Refrigerate 10-12 hours. Serve in chilled cups topped with fresh shrimp.

Serves 4.

Creamy Clam Chowder

Shaw's Hotel, Brackley Beach, PEI

To lessen the fat content, we also tested this recipe substituting light cream for heavy cream. While the soup was not as rich, it retained its wonderful flavour.

½ cup (125 mL) celery, chopped
½ cup (125 mL) onion, chopped
½ cup (125 mL) butter
3 tbsp (45 mL) all-purpose flour
2 cups (500 mL) milk
½ cup (125 mL) heavy cream (35% M.F.) or light
  cream (10% M.F.)
2 tbsp (30 mL) powdered chicken stock base
1 lb (450 g) clam meat and liquor
1 cup (250 mL) pre-cooked potatoes diced
2 tbsp (30 mL) pimento, chopped
2 tbsp (30 mL) fresh parsley, chopped

In a large saucepan, sauté the celery and onion in butter until tender, being careful not to allow the vegetables to brown. Whisk in the flour to form a roux and incorporate milk, cream and chicken stock, stirring constantly. Add clams and liquor, potatoes, pimento and parsley and cook over medium heat until hot and slightly thickened. Do not boil.

Serves 6-8.

Atlantic Blue Mussel Chowder

What a wonderful way to utilize the Maritimes' famous mussels! The subtle flavour of this golden chowder is enhanced by the addition of curry.

2 lb (900 g) fresh mussels
½ cup (125 mL) dry white wine
¼ cup (50 mL) shallots, finely chopped
⅓ cup (75 mL) onion, finely chopped
a few sprigs of parsley and dill
1 small bay leaf
2 tbsp (30 mL) butter
½ cup (125 mL) julienned celery
½ cup (125 mL) julienned carrot
2 cups (500 mL) fish stock
¾ cup (175 mL) heavy cream (35% M.F.)
1 egg yolk, beaten
1 tbsp (15 mL) curry powder (or to taste)
salt and freshly ground pepper to taste

Scrub and debeard the mussels, discarding any that are open or have broken shells. In a large pot bring to a boil wine, shallots, onion, parsley, dill and bay leaf. Add mussels and steam, covered, for 5 minutes or until they open. Strain cooking liquid through a fine mesh sieve and reserve. Discard any mussels that do not fully open. Remove mussels from shells and reserve.

In a separate heavy-bottomed saucepan, melt butter and sauté celery and carrots until softened. Remove with a slotted spoon and reserve. Add fish stock and mussel liquid to saucepan; bring to a boil and reduce by half. Add cream, mussels and julienned vegetables and remove from heat. Stir a small amount of hot mixture into beaten egg yolk, return to hot mixture. Add curry powder, season with salt and pepper and return to serving temperature, being careful not to boil.

Serves 4.

Mediterranean Seafood Stew

Nemo's Restaurant, Halifax, NS

Brian Trainor of Nemo's tells us that this dish served with fresh crusty bread makes a delicious full-bodied entrée. He suggests preparing the tomato broth ahead to enhance the flavour.

½ tbsp (8 mL) vegetable oil
¼ medium onion, chopped
1 large garlic clove minced
3 oz (100 g) fresh spinach, chopped
1 tsp (5 mL) fresh coriander (optional)
salt and pepper to taste
7 cups (1.5 L) crushed tomatoes
1 tbsp (15 mL) sugar
½ tsp (2 mL) jalapeño pepper seeded and finely
  chopped
3 cups (750 mL) fish stock
⅔ cup (150 mL) water
½ tsp (2 mL) crushed fennel seed
1 lb (450 g) fresh mussels, scrubbed and
  debearded
2 lb (900 g) haddock fillets, bite size pieces
¾ lb (375 g) scallops
¾ lb (375 g) large shrimp, peeled and deveined
½ lb (225 g) fresh clam meat
fresh parsley and lemon slices to garnish

In a large stock pot, heat oil over high heat and sauté onion and garlic until softened but not browned. Add spinach, season with coriander, salt and pepper and lower heat. Add tomatoes, sugar, jalapeño peppers and stock; simmer, stirring occasionally, for 30 minutes. Refrigerate broth for up to three days to enhance the flavour.

Reheat tomato broth over low heat. In a large saucepan bring ⅔ cup water and fennel seeds to a boil over medium heat. Add mussels, cover and steam 3 minutes. Add haddock, scallops, shrimp and clam meat, bring back to a boil and steam for an additional 2 minutes or until the mussels are open. Remove seafood from poaching liquid and add to tomato broth, discarding any mussels that have not opened.

Serve in shallow soup bowls garnished with fresh parsley and lemon slices.

Serves 6-8 generously.

Thai Crab Noodle Soup

All Seasons Café, Nelson, BC

The red chilies in Thai cooking are hot, but not overpowering. If you want more heat, consider adding a touch of red curry paste to the soup component. Whether you like it hot or hotter, enjoy!

14-oz (398-mL) can coconut cream
1 cup (250 mL) chicken stock
1½ tsp (7 mL) grated ginger root
1 stalk lemon grass, bruised
3 Kaffir lime leaves* (or 1 tsp/5 mL lime zest)
1 tsp (5 mL) fish sauce
1 tsp (5 mL) brown sugar
2 baby bok choy
3 oz (100 g) dried egg noodles
1 tbsp (15 mL) peanut oil
1 lb (450 g) crab meat
1 medium red Thai chili, seeded and thinly sliced
1 tbsp (15 mL) fresh lime juice
¼ cup (60 mL) chopped cilantro
lime slices, as garnish

In a saucepan, combine coconut cream, chicken stock, ginger root, lemon grass, lime leaves, fish sauce and brown sugar; bring to a simmer and cook 5 minutes. Strain; return to saucepan and keep warm; do not boil.

Trim bok choy; separate leaves and wash. In a saucepan with salted water, simmer bok choy until cooked. Drain; reserve and keep warm. In another saucepan, bring salted water to boil; add noodles and cook 2-3 minutes. Remove from heat, cover, and let stand until soft; strain before serving.

Heat peanut oil in a skillet; add crab and chili and toss until heated through. Drizzle lime over crab and sprinkle with cilantro. Toss to combine.

To serve: In centre of large soup bowls, place bok choy, twist noodles over bok choy and top with crab mixture. Pour soup around, garnish with additional cilantro and accompany with extra slices of lime.

Serves 4-6.

*Kaffir lime leaves are found in Asian markets.

Huron County Lobster Chowder

Little Inn of Bayfield, Bayfield, ON

Huron County, Ontario, is famous for its beans, which are exported worldwide. The chefs at the Little Inn of Bayfield use a variety of these local beans in their chowder recipe. We have tested the recipe using commercial pre-cooked beans. If you are fortunate enough to obtain fresh local beans, pre-cook them in advance and add to the recipe, as directed.

2 qt (2 L) water

2 cups (500 mL) sauvignon blanc wine

1 fennel, bulb diced, stalks sliced and leaves minced

2 dozen clams in shell

1 whole lobster (at least 2 lb/1 kg)

4 oz (125 g) bacon, diced

1 onion, diced

1 large carrot, peeled and diced

2 medium potatoes, peeled and cubed

14-oz (430-mL) can diced plum tomatoes

½ tsp (2 mL) each thyme and marjoram

¼ tsp (1 mL) cayenne pepper

2 shallots, chopped

2 garlic cloves, minced

¼ cup (60 mL) chopped parsley

1½ cups (375 mL) cooked beans of choice (pinto, kidney, cannellini, etc.)

2 tbsp (30 mL) anise-flavoured liqueur (Pernod, anisette, etc.)

In a stockpot, bring water, wine and chopped fennel stalks to a boil. Add clams and cook until they open, about 5 minutes. Remove clams with a slotted spoon. When cool, remove clam meat and slice in strips; reserve.

Add lobster to stockpot and bring back to a boil; lower heat to medium and cook 12-15 minutes. Remove lobster and cool under cold water. When cool enough to handle, break apart and remove meat. Discard stomach sac. Cut meat in chunks and reserve. Lightly crush shells; return to stockpot and bring to a simmer.

In a skillet, sauté bacon until browned; add onion and shallot and sauté until translucent. Add carrot, diced fennel bulb and potato; cook 10 minutes, stirring frequently. Add tomatoes, thyme, marjoram, cayenne, salt, pepper, garlic and beans; stir to combine.

Strain stock and return to stockpot; add bacon and vegetable mixture and simmer 30-40 minutes. Add clams, lobster, parsley, chopped fennel leaves and liqueur; bring to serving temperature and adjust seasoning. Serve with bread of choice.

Serves 6.

Lobster Bisque

C Restaurant, Vancouver, BC

Creative chefs love to introduce personal ingredients into traditional recipes. Executive Chef Robert Clark enhances the delicate lobster flavour of his bisque with a subtle infusion of exotic spices—the results are spectacular!

2 lb (1 kg) cooked lobster bodies and claw shells
½ cup (125 mL) butter
1 small carrot, chopped
1 small stalk celery, chopped
1 red pepper, chopped
1 red onion, chopped
1 head fennel, chopped
1 tomato, chopped
5 garlic cloves, minced
4 bay leaves
4 star anise, toasted*
4 whole cloves, toasted*
1 tbsp (15 mL) annatto seed paste** (or a pinch of saffron)
1 tbsp (15 mL) white peppercorns
1 tbsp (15 mL) maple syrup
1 cup (250 mL) white wine
½ cup (125 mL) brandy
8 cups (2 L) heavy cream (35% M.F.)

Remove the lobsters' sand sacs (the organ located behind the eyes); break up lobster bodies and claws into medium-sized pieces. Reserve.

Heat butter in a large saucepan over medium-low heat. Add vegetables and spices and sweat, covered, until vegetables are softened and begin to colour, about 5 minutes. Add lobster shells and maple syrup and cook, uncovered, until they begin to stick and there is no moisture, about 8 minutes. Raise heat to medium-high, add wine and brandy and deglaze, stirring frequently, until liquid evaporates.

Reduce heat to medium, add cream and slowly bring to a simmer, being careful not to boil. Remove from heat, cool to room temperature and then refrigerate for 2 hours, allowing flavours to blend. Bring back to room temperature and strain through a fine-mesh strainer. Return bisque to saucepan, bring back to a low simmer and cook for 2 minutes. Serve immediately.

Serves 6.

*To toast spices: heat a heavy skillet over medium heat until hot. Add spices and toast, stirring frequently, until fragrant, about 2 to 5 minutes.

**Annatto seed paste is a derivative of the achiote seed and is commonly used in Mexican cookery for its flavour and yellow colouring. It can be found in Mexican food stores.

Preparing lobster for Fresh
Atlantic Lobster Soufflé, p.58

Luncheon

These luncheon and "one-dish" meals are perfect for people with busy lifestyles. Crab Crèpes with Lemon Caper Sauce and Pasta Alberoni, served with a salad, are excellent choices for a light dinner.

Lobster Ravioli in Lemon Cream

Step'n Out Eclectic Cuisine, Winnipeg, MB

Rich, yet delicately flavourful, this luncheon dish will delight your palate and bring accolades from your guests.

2 eggs
1 tbsp (15 mL) finely minced onion
1 tbsp (15 mL) finely minced garlic
10 oz (300 g) lobster meat, chopped
⅓ cup (75 mL) chopped fresh parsley
⅓ cup (75 mL) chopped fresh basil
zest of 2 lemons
½ cup (125 mL) breadcrumbs
1 tsp (5 mL) honey
salt and pepper
12 oz (1 pkg) gyoza (dumpling) wrappers
egg wash (1 beaten egg + ½tsp/2 mL water)
1 pkg (375 g) fresh spinach
cream sauce (recipe follows)
gremolata (recipe follows)

In a medium-sized bowl, whisk eggs. Add onion, garlic, lobster, parsley, lemon zest, breadcrumbs, honey, salt and pepper; mix to combine. Mixture should be firm; add additional bread crumbs, if necessary.

If using a dough press, place wrapper on press, brush edges with egg wash and place 1 tbsp (15 mL) lobster mixture in centre of wrapper. Fold dough press to form a furled crescent shape. If shaping by hand, place wrapper on work surface, brush edges with egg wash and centre 1 tbsp (15 mL) lobster mixture. Fold in half, forming a crescent shape, and crimp firmly to seal. Place ravioli on baking sheet covered with a damp towel. Repeat process with the rest of the mixture.

In a large saucepan two-thirds full of boiling salted water, cook 4-5 ravioli at a time until they rise to the top and are cooked, about 4 minutes. With a slotted spoon, remove ravioli to an oiled baking sheet and cool. Repeat until all are cooked.

Add ravioli to warm cream sauce and bring to serving temperature. In a saucepan of boiling water, cook spinach until wilted, about 1 minute; drain well.

To serve: centre spinach on 6 warmed serving plates; top with ravioli and spoon additional cream sauce around. Garnish with sprinkling of gremolata.

Serves 6.

Cream Sauce

1 tsp (5 mL) olive oil
2 tbsp (30 mL) minced onion
2 tbsp (30 mL) roasted garlic*, minced
½ cup (125 mL) white wine
2 tbsp (30 mL) butter, cubed
juice of 2 lemons
2 cups (500 mL) heavy cream (35% M.F.)
salt and pepper

In a skillet, heat olive oil; add onion and cook until translucent. Stir in roasted garlic and deglaze pan with wine. Whisk in butter, lemon juice and cream; cook on low heat for flavours to fuse, about 10 minutes. Remove from heat, cover and let rest another 10 minutes. Strain through a fine sieve and return to skillet; adjust seasoning with salt and pepper to taste.

Gremolata (garnish)

2 tbsp (30 mL) chopped fresh basil
2 tbsp (30 mL) chopped fresh parsley
zest of 1 lemon

In a bowl, toss together basil, parsley and lemon zest.

*To roast garlic: Remove outer skin from whole garlic bulbs and trim ½ inch (1 cm) from the pointed end. Pour a small amount of olive oil over the cut ends and bake, covered, in preheated 375°F (190°C) oven until cloves are browned and soft, about 30 minutes. Squeeze individual cloves from bulb. Store refrigerated 3-4 days or freeze.

Lemon Steamed Mussels

Innlet Café, Mahone Bay, NS

This is about as good as it gets. Steamed mussels, crisp shredded vegetables and tart lemon slices— you will have your guests begging for the recipe.

3 lb (1.5 kg) cultivated mussels
6 tbsp (90 mL) unsalted butter
2 tbsp (30 mL) all-purpose flour
4 tbsp (60 mL) grated carrot
2 tbsp (30 mL) chopped green onion
2 tbsp (30 mL) chopped parsley
1 garlic clove, minced
¼ tsp (1 mL) pepper
¼ cup (50 mL) water
1 lemon, thinly sliced

Scrub and debeard mussels in cold running water, discarding any that are open or have broken shells. Combine all ingredients except mussels in a large saucepan and bring to a boil, stirring constantly. Add mussels and stir to coat them evenly with sauce. Cover and steam for 5-7 minutes, being careful not to overcook. Remove mussels to two large bowls, discarding any that have not opened. Top with sauce.

Serves 2.

Lobster Club Sandwich

The ultimate lobster sandwich—served
Maritime-style with a side of coleslaw and fries!

3 slices of white bread, toasted
3 strips bacon, cooked crisp and drained
4 oz (125 g) lobster meat
shredded lettuce
thin tomato slices
mayonnaise

Spread first slice of toast with mayonnaise and
cover with lettuce, tomato, and bacon. Cover
with second slice of toast, spread with
mayonnaise and lobster meat. Spread
mayonnaise on one side of the third slice of
toast and place on top of the sandwich. To
serve, cut in quarters and secure with
toothpicks. Garnish as desired.

Serves 1.

Lobster Roll

Mountain Gap Inn, Smiths Cove, NS

This traditional Maritime lobster roll is served with fries and coleslaw. We tested the sandwich using Cecilia Bowden's roll recipe from the Compass Rose, Grand Manan Island.

3 cups (750 mL) cooked lobster meat, in
  bite-sized pieces
¼ cup (60 mL) celery, chopped fine
mayonnaise
salt and pepper to taste
shredded lettuce
4 "lobster" rolls (recipe follows)

Fold together lobster and celery with just enough mayonnaise to bind them. Season with salt and pepper. Split four rolls almost through and toast lightly. Place lettuce on rolls and fill with lobster mixture.

Serves 4.

"Lobster" Rolls
The Compass Rose, Grand Manan Island, NB

1 tbsp (15 mL) dry yeast
1 tsp (5 mL) granulated sugar
½ cup (125 mL) lukewarm water
⅓ cup (75 mL) granulated sugar (2nd amount)
1 tsp (5 mL) salt
⅓ cup (75 mL) oil
1⅔ cups (400 mL) warm water

5-6 cups (1.3-1.5 L) all-purpose flour
1 tbsp (15 mL) butter

Dissolve yeast and 1 teaspoon (5 mL) sugar in lukewarm water and let rise to at least 1 cup (250 mL) in volume. Combine sugar (2nd amount), salt, oil and warm water in a large bowl and whisk briskly. Add yeast mixture to other liquids and beat until smooth. Gradually add flour, a cupful at a time, beating after each addition, until you need to use your hands to combine the remainder.

Turn out on a flour-covered surface and knead until smooth and slightly sticky, about 5 minutes. Place dough in a greased bowl and turn to cover with oil. Cover and let rise for 45 minutes in a warm, draft-free place.

Punch down and shape into 12 oblong rolls. Place on a greased baking sheet, cover loosely and let rise again for 45 minutes.

Preheat oven to 375°F (190°C). Bake rolls for 12-15 minutes, until slightly golden. Remove from oven, brush tops with butter and cool on wire racks.

Yields 12 "lobster" rolls.

Lobster on Potato Pancakes with Sour Cream Sauce

Dufferin Inn and San Martello Dining Room
Saint John, NB

Owners Margret and Axel Begner give a European flavour to Atlantic lobster with these potato pancakes accompanied by sour cream sauce.

3 medium-sized potatoes, peeled
1 tbsp (15 mL) all-purpose flour
1 egg, slightly beaten
pinch of salt
vegetable oil for frying
1½ cups (375 mL) fresh lobster meat
sour cream sauce (recipe follows)

Grate potatoes into a large bowl. Stir in flour and beaten egg. Heat a skillet and brush with a small amount of oil. Drop heaping tablespoons of potato mixture onto hot skillet and fry pancakes until golden brown on one side. Flip pancakes, press with a spatula to flatten, and fry until golden. Remove from skillet, set on paper towels to remove any excess oil and keep warm.

To serve, arrange pancakes on individual plates, top with lobster and nap with sour cream sauce.

Serves 4-6.

Sour Cream Sauce

½ cup (125 mL) sour cream
½ tsp (2 mL) prepared horseradish
½ tsp (2 mL) lemon juice
pinch of sugar
1 green onion, thinly sliced
salt and pepper to taste

Combine all ingredients in a small bowl and whisk until blended. Refrigerate.

Lobster Toast Points

Inn on the Lake, Fall River, NS

At the inn, this dish is served with fresh parsley and a side salad. It provides an ample luncheon serving or light dinner entrée.

¼ lb (125 g) fresh mushrooms, diced
8–12 oz (225–375 g) cooked lobster meat, in bite-sized chunks
3 tbsp (45 mL) grated carrot
2½ tbsp (35 mL) fish stock
½ tsp (2 mL) sweet Hungarian paprika (or to taste)
1 cup (250 mL) heavy cream (35% M.F.)
¼ lb (125 g) cheddar cheese, grated
4 thick slices white bread
8 sprigs fresh parsley, chopped

Combine mushrooms, lobster, carrot, stock, paprika and cream in a large saucepan and cook over medium heat until slightly thickened. Add cheese and stir until melted. Toast bread and cut in wedges. Serve lobster mixture spooned over toast and garnished with fresh parsley.

Serves 4.

Crab Crèpes with Lemon Caper Sauce

This impressive luncheon dish is both inexpensive and easy to prepare. We found that the lemon caper sauce is delicious served with other seafood, as well.

2 tbsp (30 mL) butter
1 tbsp (15 mL) vegetable oil
1 small onion, diced
1 small green pepper, diced
1 garlic clove, crushed
4 oz (125 g) cooked ham, finely chopped
8 oz (225 g) crab meat
1 tbsp (15 mL) brandy (optional)
salt and freshly ground pepper to taste
crèpes to serve 4 (recipe follows)
lemon caper sauce (recipe follows)

Heat butter and oil in a skillet; add onion, green pepper and garlic and sauté until vegetables are softened but not browned. Add ham and crab meat and cook for 1 minute; stir in brandy. Remove from heat, add salt and pepper to taste and reserve.

Preheat oven to 350°F (180°C). To assemble: divide crab filling among crèpes and roll up, enclosing the ends. Place seam side down in a greased shallow baking dish, cover with foil and bake for 15 minutes. Serve with warm lemon caper sauce.

Serves 4.

Basic Crèpe Recipe

The crèpes may be made in advance. Separate them with waxed paper, wrap them tightly in foil and freeze. To thaw, simply remove quantity needed and bring to room temperature.

2 eggs
1 cup (250 mL) milk
¾ cup (175 mL) all-purpose flour
pinch of salt

Whisk together eggs and milk. Add flour and salt and continue beating until the batter is smooth. Rest batter for 1 hour.

Brush a non-stick skillet with a little vegetable oil and heat on medium. Add enough batter to barely cover the bottom of the pan (scant ¼ cup/50 mL) and cook for approximately 30 seconds. Flip crèpe and cook for another 15 seconds. Repeat, setting crèpes aside to cool.

Makes approximately 1 dozen large or 16 medium crèpes.

Lemon Caper Sauce

1 cup (250 mL) chicken broth
⅓ cup (75 mL) butter
3 tbsp (45 mL) fresh lemon juice
1 egg yolk, beaten
1 tbsp (15 mL) water
2 tsp (10 mL) cornstarch
1 tbsp (15 mL) capers, drained and chopped
white pepper to taste

Bring broth, butter and lemon juice to a boil over medium-high heat, stirring until the butter melts. Reduce heat to low. Blend egg, water and cornstarch until creamy. Stir small amount of hot mixture into egg, add to hot mixture and cook, stirring constantly until thickened. Do not boil. Remove from heat, stir in capers and season to taste with pepper. Serve warm.

Fresh Atlantic Lobster Soufflé

Acton's Grill and Café, Wolfville, NS

At Acton's, this soufflé is accompanied by assorted greens dressed with a fresh herb vinaigrette. Always serve a soufflé straight from the oven before it collapses.

16 cups (4 L) water
1 tbsp (15 mL) salt
1 medium onion, peeled and halved
1 medium carrot, peeled and diced
2 stalks celery
2 small bay leaves
4 whole cloves
6 whole allspice
2-3 tomatoes, cut in chunks
1 tbsp (15 mL) paprika
1½ lb (650 g) lobster
2 tbsp (30 mL) unsalted butter
2 tbsp (30 mL) all-purpose flour
1 cup (250 mL) reserved lobster stock
¼ cup (60 mL) heavy cream (35% M.F.), warmed
¼ tsp (1 mL) lemon juice
1 tbsp (15 mL) brandy
6 whole eggs, separated
salt and freshly ground white pepper to taste

Pour water into large stockpot. Add salt, onion, carrot, celery, bay, cloves, allspice, tomatoes and paprika. Bring to a boil; reduce heat and simmer 15 minutes. Return to full boil, add lobster, cover and cook 15 minutes. Remove lobster from pot and set aside to cool. Keep stock hot.

Twist the tail and claws from the lobster body. Remove meat from shells, cut into small chunks and reserve. Split body in half, place in stockpot and return to a boil. Reduce heat and simmer 1 hour. Strain, discarding solids and reserving stock.

Preheat oven to 400°F (200°C). In a heavy saucepan, melt butter and whisk in flour. Cook over low heat for 1 minute, then add cream and 1 cup (250 mL) reserved lobster stock. Bring to a boil, whisking constantly until sauce thickens. Remove from heat; whisk in lemon juice, brandy and egg yolks. Add lobster meat, season with salt and pepper and set aside.

Butter and lightly flour a 2-quart (2-L) soufflé dish. Beat egg whites until stiff, but not dry, then gently fold in the lobster mixture. Pour into soufflé dish and bake for 15-20 minutes, until puffed and browned. Serve immediately.

Serves 4.

Quaco Inn Lobster and Pasta

Quaco Inn, St. Martins, NB

The addition of lime gives a most delightful flavour to this dish! We served it on a bed of fresh fettucini.

1 tbsp (15 mL) olive oil
2-3 garlic cloves, minced
12 oz (375 g) lobster meat, in bite-sized pieces
1 tbsp (15 mL) fresh basil, chopped (or 1 tsp/
  5 mL dried)
1 tbsp (15 mL) fresh chives, chopped (or 1 tsp/
  5 mL dried)
1 tbsp fresh oregano (or 1 tsp/5 mL dried)
2-3 fresh tomatoes, cut in wedges
19-oz (540-mL) can Italian-style plum tomatoes
zest and juice of 1 lime
salt and pepper to taste
¼ cup (60 mL) freshly grated Parmesan cheese
pasta of choice to serve 4

Heat olive oil in a heavy-bottomed saucepan, add garlic and sauté until softened, being careful not to brown. Stir in lobster and sauté until heated through. Add herbs, fresh and canned tomatoes, lime juice and zest. Season with salt and pepper. Stir in Parmesan cheese and return to serving temperature.

Cook pasta until *al dente*. Drain and serve topped with sauce and garnished with fresh herbs and additional Parmesan cheese, if desired.

Serves 4.

Lobster Linguini

Blomidon Inn, Wolfville, NS

We questioned the chef at the Blomidon Inn on the quantity of horseradish in this recipe and were assured that, indeed, it was the proper amount. This delicious, easily-prepared lobster entrée has an unforgettable flavour.

1 tbsp (15 mL) butter
12 oz (375 g) lobster meat
⅔ cup (150 mL) chopped tomatoes
4 tbsp (60 mL) creamed horseradish
¼ cup (60 mL) dry white wine
3 cups (750 mL) heavy cream (35% M.F.)
¼ cup (60 mL) chopped green onions
salt and pepper to taste
1 lb (450 g) fresh linguini pasta

Heat butter in a heavy skillet on medium-high; sauté lobster, tomatoes and horseradish until tomatoes are softened. Remove lobster and tomatoes with a slotted spoon and reserve.

Deglaze skillet with wine. Add cream, bring to a boil and reduce to a slightly-thickened sauce consistency. Add green onions, reserved lobster and tomatoes; season with salt and pepper.

In a large pot of boiling salted water, cook pasta until *al dente* (tender yet firm). Drain pasta and serve on warmed plates topped with lobster cream sauce.

Serves 4-6.

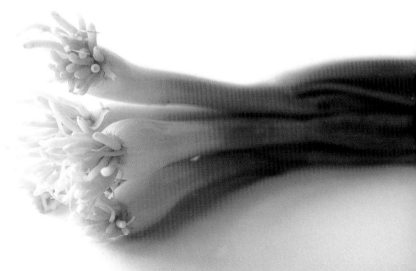

Mussels in Blue Cheese Sauce

Maestro SVP, Montreal, QC

There are many ways to serve steamed mussels, and we are sure this recipe will become a favourite. Chef Yves Therrien serves his mussels in large bowls with a side of Belgium fries and mayonnaise.

2 lb (1 kg) fresh mussels, rinsed and debearded
1 cup (250 mL) mixed vegetables, julienned
½ cup (125 mL) heavy cream (35% M.F.)
½ cup (125 mL) fish stock
¼ cup (60 mL) white wine
4 oz (125 g) blue cheese, crumbled

Clean mussels and discard any with broken shells. Combine all ingredients in a large saucepan and bring to a boil. Stir to coat mussels, reduce heat and steam until mussels open, about 6 minutes. Remove any mussels that have not opened. Pour sauce over mussels.

Serves 2.

Lobster in Vanilla Cream Sauce

Edgewater Manor Restaurant, Stoney Creek, ON

At Edgewater Manor Restaurant, the chef uses a vanilla bean to infuse the flavour of this cream sauce. He simmers the bean in the cream mixture for 5 minutes, then splits it and scrapes the seeds into the sauce, removing the pod. For the ease of the home cook, we offer simpler directions using pure vanilla extract.

2 tbsp (30 mL) butter
2 tbsp (30 mL) chopped shallots
¼ cup (60 mL) dry white wine
2 cups (500 mL) heavy cream (35% M.F.)
1 tsp (5 mL) pure vanilla extract
1 lb (450 g) cooked lobster tails and claws,
   shelled and drained
salt and pepper
4 pre-baked puff pastry cups

Melt butter over medium heat and sauté shallots until transparent. Deglaze the pan with wine and reduce by half. Stir in cream and vanilla and bring to a boil. Reduce heat and simmer until sauce has reduced by half and thickened slightly. Stir in lobster pieces and season with salt and pepper. Serve in puff pastry cups.

Serves 4.

Barbecued Lobster with Red Pepper and Lime Butter, p.68

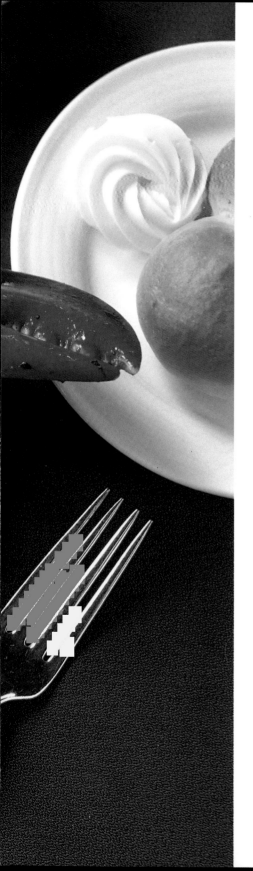

Main Courses

Behold, an array of dishes suitable for family gatherings
or gala entertaining! From Dalvay by the Sea's
Barbecued Lobster with Red Pepper and Lime Butter to
the elegant Coquille St. Jacques from Stories Restaurant
at Halliburton House Inn, there is something for
everyone's taste.

Barbecued Lobster with
Red Pepper and Lime Butter

Dalvay by the Sea, Dalvay, PEI

This lobster recipe, with its subtle roasted red pepper and lime, provides a completely different flavour from boiled lobster. To complete your feast, Chef Richard Kemp, of Dalvay, includes his Jamaican Coleslaw recipe, which he serves as an accompaniment.

4 lobsters (1 -1½ lb/450 -650 g each)
1 red bell pepper
2 tbsp (30 mL) oil
1 cup (250 mL) butter, softened
juice and zest of 2 limes
salt and pepper to taste
pinch of cayenne pepper
½ cup (125 mL) olive oil
2 garlic cloves, chopped
juice of 1 lemon
½ cup (125 mL) chopped chives
½ cup (125mL) chopped cilantro
coarsely ground black pepper
lemon wedges, as garnish

Bring a large pot of salted water to a boil; plunge lobsters in for 4 -6 minutes to blanch. Remove lobsters and cool until you can handle them. Cut in half lengthwise, remove viscera, and crack claws.

Preheat oven to 425°F (220°C). Brush red pepper with oil, place on a baking sheet and roast for 15 minutes, turning several times. Remove from oven and cool. Carefully peel off pepper skin, remove seeds and chop the pepper. Place softened butter, red pepper, lime juice and zest in a blender and process until smooth. Season with salt, pepper and cayenne. Set aside at room temperature.

Prepare marinade by combining olive oil, garlic, lemon juice, chives, coriander and black pepper. Rub thoroughly over lobster and let stand for 20 minutes. Barbecue lobster flesh-side down on a hot grill until golden. Turn, brush flesh with red pepper butter and cook, shell side down for another 6-8 minutes, allowing the lobster to braise in its own juices. Arrange lobster on warm plates, top with remaining red pepper butter and serve with a large spoonful of jamaican coleslaw (recipe follows) and a garnish of lemon wedges.

Jamaican Coleslaw

¼ head red cabbage
¼ head chinese cabbage
1 red onion
2 stalks celery
1 large carrot
1 garlic clove, minced
½ tsp (2 mL) ground cumin
½ tsp (2 mL) ground coriander seeds
½ tsp (2 mL) curry powder
½ tsp (2 mL) Dijon mustard
juice of 2 limes
¼ cup (50 mL) red wine vinegar
1 cup (250 mL) olive oil
salt and pepper to taste

Finely slice the cabbages, onion, celery and carrot. Set aside in a large bowl. Place remaining ingredients, except salt and pepper, in a blender and process. Pour sauce over vegetables and mix well. Season with salt and pepper.

Serves 4.

Pan-seared Scallops with Black Olive Couscous, Basil Purée and Tomato Olive Broth

The Inn at Bay Fortune, Bay Fortune, PEI

Chef Michael Smith has a penchant for creating exotic entrées. Don't be intimidated! If you read through the recipe and prepare each segment separately, it is not difficult and the presentation is stunning.

1-1¼ lb (450-550 g) large scallops
butter for searing
tomato olive broth (recipe follows)
basil purée (recipe follows)
black olive couscous (recipe follows)

Heat a heavy-bottomed skillet over high heat. Add butter and scallops and sear until the scallops are just cooked.

Prepare tomato olive broth, basil purée and black olive couscous.

Tomato Olive Broth
1 large or 2 medium vine-ripened tomatoes
¼ cup (60 mL) extra virgin olive oil
salt and pepper to taste

Purée tomato and olive oil in a blender until very smooth, season with salt and pepper. Reserve and gently heat before serving.

Basil Purée
1 cup (250 mL) densely-packed fresh basil leaves
¼ cup (60 mL) extra virgin olive oil

Purée basil and olive oil in a blender until very smooth. Reserve and refrigerate.

Black Olive Couscous
1⅞ cups (450 mL) water
1 cup (250 mL) black olives (preferably kalamata), chopped
¼ cup (60 mL) extra virgin olive oil
½ tsp (2 mL) salt
1 cup (250 mL) couscous grain

Bring water, olives, oil and salt to a boil. Stir in couscous and return to a boil; immediately cover and remove from heat. Let sit for 5 minutes. Place in individual molds, if desired, and serve immediately.

Assemble entrée on a platter or individual serving plates. Place black olive couscous in centre of dish, then arrange scallops around the couscous. Dot each scallop with basil purée and serve drizzled with warmed tomato olive broth.

Serves 4.

Fresh Steamed Lobster

This failproof recipe for freshly steamed lobster was given to us by innkeepers in Lunenburg, NS. We suggest you remove the rubber bands from the lobster claws before cooking, as they transfer a rubber taste to the lobster meat.

2 lobsters (1 lb/450 g each)
½ cup (125 mL) melted butter
1 lemon, sliced in wedges
romaine leaves, as garnish
parsley sprigs, as garnish

Use a steamer pot or place a vegetable steamer in an appropriately sized pot with enough water to cover the bottom of the steamer by 1 inch (2.5 cm). Bring the water to a hard boil, place lobsters in the steamer and cover. Cooking time will vary depending on the size of the lobsters, but a 1-pound (0.5-kg) lobster is cooked in 15 minutes.

When cooked, remove the lobster from the pot and briefly cool under cold water. For ease of eating, crack the lobster in the kitchen: place the lobster upside down; take a cleaver and place the point at the beginning of the tail; slice down the middle, breaking right through the outer shell. With the lobster still on its back, bring the cleaver sharply down on each claw and twist sideways, forcing the claw shell apart.

For presentation, put two romaine leaves on a plate and place the lobster on top, with the front covering the stems of the romaine. Between the claws place a small bowl of melted butter. Position two lemon wedges where the claws join the body and parsley sprigs between the lemons and along the cut made in the tail. Take a paper towel dipped in a small amount of the melted butter and rub over the lobster shell. *Bon appetit!*

Serves 2.

Astice con Funghi (Lobster with Wild Mushrooms)

Da Maurizio, Halifax, NS

The addition of wild portobello and porcini mushrooms gives this Northern Italian entrée a delicate woodsy flavour.

1 oz (30 g) dried porcini mushrooms
½ cup (125 mL) white wine
4 lobsters (1½ lb/650 g each)
cooking stock (recipe follows)
¼ cup (60 mL) butter
1 small onion, diced
12 oz (375 g) fresh portobello mushrooms, stems removed
2 cups (500 mL) tomato sauce
6 fresh basil leaves (or ¼ tsp/1 mL dried)
salt and pepper to taste

Soak porcini mushrooms in white wine and let stand for 30 minutes.

Prepare lobsters according to cooking stock directions (see below). Carefully remove meat from claws and tails; keep warm.

In a large skillet, melt butter, add onion and sauté until translucent. Slice portobello mushrooms ¼ inch (0.5 cm) thick and add to onions. Sauté until tender, approximately 5 minutes. Add porcini mushrooms, wine, tomato sauce and basil, cooking until sauce is reduced and slightly thickened. Season with salt and pepper.

To serve, spoon sauce onto four plates and arrange lobster on top in its original shape.

Serves 4.

Stock
8 cups (2 L) water
4 tbsp (60 mL) coarse salt
1 medium onion, quartered
1 stalk celery, chopped
1 medium carrot, chopped
2 bay leaves
1 sprig parsley
1 sprig thyme
1 lemon, quartered

In a large stockpot, combine all ingredients. Bring to a boil, reduce heat and simmer for 15 minutes. Return to a hard boil, plunge lobsters into water and bring back to a boil. Reduce heat and cook lobsters for 16 minutes. Remove lobsters and cool to room temperature.

Lobster Truffle Gnocchi with Lobster Emulsion

Diva at the Met, Vancouver, BC

Truffle oil with its earthy essence has a very concentrated flavour and should be used in moderation. This is one instance where "a little is heavenly" and "more is not better." You will find truffle oil in specialty food markets.

2 live lobsters (1½ lb/650 g each)
4 tbsp (60 mL) butter, divided
⅓ cup (75 mL) diced celeriac
¼ cup (60 mL) chicken stock
1 tsp (5 mL) white truffle oil
gnocchi (recipe follows)
lobster emulsion (recipe follows)
white truffles, as garnish (optional)

Bring a large pot of water to a boil. Add lobsters, bring back to a boil and cook for 2 minutes. Remove lobsters; pull off tails and claws, reserving tails for another use. Return claws to boiling water and cook for 5 minutes longer. Lift claws from water and, while warm, remove shells with scissors, keeping the claw meat in one piece. Reserve and refrigerate claw meat. Cut lobster bodies in half; discard eyes and stomach sac and rinse well under water to clean. Break shells and bodies into smaller pieces and reserve for emulsion.

Prepare gnocchi and lobster emulsion.

Place lobster claw meat on a small baking sheet and brush with 1 tbsp (15 mL) softened butter. Place in preheated 350°F (180°C) oven for 5 minutes to warm. In a skillet, heat 1 tbsp (15 mL) butter, add celeriac and sauté until soft, about 4 minutes. Add reserved gnocchi, chicken stock and remaining butter. Simmer until stock has slightly thickened and coats gnocchi. Add truffle oil and adjust seasoning.

To serve: divide gnocchi among 4 plates; top gnocchi with a lobster claw that has been sliced on the diagonal. Whisk the lobster emulsion to create a froth and gently spoon around gnocchi. If using truffles, shave slices on top to garnish plates.

Serves 4.

Gnocchi
2 medium russet potatoes
½-¾ cup (125-175 mL) all-purpose flour
2 egg yolks, beaten
1 tsp (5 mL) salt
olive oil

Bake potatoes in a preheated 375°F/190°C oven for 1 hour or until completely cooked. Peel potatoes while still warm, and mash or press through a ricer. Place warm potatoes in a bowl and make a well in the centre. To the well, add ½ cup (125 mL) flour, egg yolks and salt; gently fold with a wooden spoon until ingredients are incorporated and the mixture is not sticky. Use additional flour if the potato mixture is on the wet side. Roll the dough into a ball and portion into three pieces.

On a floured work-surface, roll each piece of dough into ⅛-inch (0.25-cm) strips and cut into ½-inch (1-cm) pieces. Drop pieces into a large pot of boiling water and cook until the gnocchi float to the top. Remove gnocchi with a slotted spoon, place on a baking sheet and drizzle with olive oil. Cool and reserve.

Lobster Emulsion

2 tomatoes, chopped
⅓ cup (75 mL) diced carrot
1½ tbsp (20 mL) fresh tarragon
2 cups (500 mL) heavy cream (35% M.F.)

In a saucepan over medium-high heat, add lobster bodies and sauté for 2 minutes; add tomatoes, carrots and tarragon and sauté for an additional 2 minutes. Add enough water to cover shells and simmer on low heat for 1 hour. Strain stock through a fine-mesh strainer into a small saucepan. Return stock to simmer and reduce to 1 cup. Add cream and simmer until reduced to 2 cups. Keep warm.

Cappesante di Chioggra
(Scallops Chioggra Style)

La Perla, Dartmouth, NS

This is one of La Perla's acclaimed authentic Northern Italian dishes. Savour the aroma of garlic, brandy and lemon, married to the subtle taste of scallops. It's a union made in heaven!

1¼ lb (575 g) large scallops
2 tsp (10 mL) coarse salt
⅓ cup (75 mL) olive oil
2-3 medium-sized garlic cloves, finely chopped
12-15 sprigs Italian parsley, finely chopped
salt and pepper to taste
¼ cup (60 mL) dry white wine
2 tbsp (30 mL) brandy, slightly warmed
juice of 1 lemon

Place scallops in cold water with salt and soak for 30 minutes. Heat oil in a large skillet over medium heat and sauté garlic and parsley for 2 minutes. Drain scallops and pat dry. Lower heat and add scallops to skillet; cover pan and cook for 3 minutes. Season with salt and pepper, add wine and cook until reduced by one-half. Add slightly warmed brandy and flambé. Drizzle with lemon juice.

Serves 4.

Lobster and Chicken Supreme

Marshlands Inn, Sackville, NB

The chefs at Marshlands Inn cut the chicken and lobster pieces in medallions and serve them alternately on the plate. Drizzled with a rich sherry-flavoured cream sauce, this dish is a perfect entrée for special occasions.

2 lobsters (1½ lb/650 g each)
5 tbsp (75mL) vegetable oil, portioned
½ cup (125 mL) sherry
1⅓ cups (325 mL) heavy cream (35% M.F.)
4 boneless chicken breasts (4 oz/125 g each)
flour, for dusting
salt and pepper to taste

Bring a large kettle of salted water to a full boil. Plunge lobsters head first into water and hold under water with a wooden spoon for 4 minutes. Remove from water and set aside until cool enough to handle.

Separate claws and tails from lobster bodies. Remove tomalley from bodies and reserve. (Tomalley is the soft olive-green liver, found in the body of the lobster. It is considered a delicacy, and can be eaten alone or incorporated into sauces.)

Crack claws and slice tails (shells and meat) into medallions. In a large skillet, heat 3 tbsp (45 mL) oil until hot and sauté lobster pieces, stirring occasionally, for 2 -3 minutes. Deglaze pan with sherry, bring to a boil; add cream and simmer for 8 -10 minutes until cooked.

Preheat oven to 400°F (200°C). Dredge chicken in flour, coating lightly. Heat 2 tbsp (30 mL) oil over high heat in a heavy ovenproof skillet and brown chicken, turning once. Place skillet in oven and bake until chicken is no longer pink in the centre (5 -7 minutes).

With a slotted spoon, remove lobster from pan. Separate meat from shells and keep warm. Return sauce to medium heat, whisk in reserved tomalley and juices and reduce until slightly thickened. Season sauce with salt and pepper. Arrange lobster and chicken on plates and top with cream sauce.

Serves 4.

Lobster Oriental

Inn on the Cove and Spa, Saint John, NB

Ross and Willa Mavis often give a New Brunswick flavour to this entrée by using blanched fiddleheads instead of broccoli or zucchini. Try it with your own choice of vegetable combinations.

2 cups (500 mL) lobster meat
2 tbsp (30 mL) canola oil
1 cup (250 mL) fresh mushrooms, sliced
1 cup (250 mL) celery, diagonally sliced
1 cup (250 mL) cauliflower florets
1 cup (250 mL) broccoli florets or sliced zucchini
1 red or yellow pepper, cubed
½ cup (125 mL) fish or chicken stock
1 tbsp (15 mL) cornstarch
1 tbsp (15 mL) cold water
1 tbsp (15 mL) soya or oyster sauce
⅛ tsp (0.5 mL) hot red pepper flakes, or to taste
salt and pepper to taste
1 tsp (5 mL) dulse flakes (optional)

Coarsely chop lobster, removing cartilage and any shell pieces; set aside. In a wok or large skillet, heat canola oil over medium-high heat. Add vegetables and stir or toss quickly for 1-2 minutes. Add broth and cover to allow vegetables to steam until crisp tender. Mix cornstarch with cold water; add soya or oyster sauce and hot pepper flakes. Stir into hot broth in wok and coat all vegetables. Add lobster and heat through. Sprinkle with dulse flakes and serve with rice or pasta.

Serves 4.

Coquille St. Jacques

Stories Restaurant at Halliburton House Inn
Halifax, NS

The chef at Stories Restaurant serves his elegant
Coquille St. Jacques in individual scallop shells
surrounded by piped duchess potatoes.

2 tbsp (30 mL) butter
1 tbsp (15 mL) lemon juice
1-1¼ lb (450-550 g) fresh Digby scallops
2 large garlic cloves, finely chopped
4 tbsp (60 mL) dry white wine
2 tbsp (30 mL) brandy or cognac
1 cup (250 mL) heavy cream (35% M.F.)
½ cup (125 mL) grated Parmesan cheese

Melt butter in a skillet over medium-high heat
and add lemon juice; sauté scallops and garlic
until scallops are springy to the touch, about 3-
5 minutes depending upon size. Remove to a
warm serving plate and reserve.

Deglaze pan with wine and brandy and any juice
that has formed under the scallops. Over medium
heat, reduce mixture to the consistency of a thick
glaze. Slowly stir in cream and simmer until sauce
becomes thick. Add scallops and return to serving
temperature. Place in individual scallop shells or a
shallow casserole. Sprinkle with Parmesan cheese
and broil until golden.

Serves 4.

Lobster Newburg

Amherst Shore Country Inn, Lorneville, NS

At the Amherst Shore Country Inn, the first person of the day to make a dinner reservation may be asked by the innkeeper to decide the menu for that evening. This entrée is often requested.

⅓ cup (75 mL) butter
4 cups (1 L) fresh lobster meat, in bite-sized pieces
generous dash of paprika
generous dash of nutmeg
½ cup (125 mL) medium-dry sherry
6 egg yolks, lightly beaten
2 cups (500 mL) heavy cream (35% M.F.)

Melt butter in the top of a double boiler over hot, but not boiling, water. Add lobster meat and sauté gently until heated through. Add paprika, nutmeg and sherry, and return to serving temperature. Blend egg yolks and cream with a wire whisk; add to the lobster and heat gently until hot and the sauce begins to thicken. Do not boil. Serve immediately in a puff pastry shell, over rice or with a medley of seasonal vegetables.

Serves 6.

Seafood Lasagna

The Compass Rose, Grand Manan Island, NB

Guests at Grand Manan's the Compass Rose are treated to spectacular seafood fresh from the docks at North Head. We tested this recipe using light cottage cheese and milk in place of the cream. While the dish was not as rich, we were delighted with the results.

10 lasagna noodles
1½ lb (650 g) mixed seafood (e.g. lobster, scallops, shrimp, crab, salmon, white fish)
1 lb (450 g) fresh spinach
4 eggs
1 lb (450 g) cottage cheese
salt and pepper to taste
⅛ tsp (0.5 mL) nutmeg
6 tbsp (90 mL) butter
1 onion, chopped
1 garlic clove, crushed
1 tbsp (15 mL) fresh dill
6 tbsp (90 mL) all-purpose flour
salt and pepper to taste
2 tbsp (30 mL) sherry
3 cups (750 mL) light cream (10% M.F.)
1 cup (250 mL) grated Swiss cheese
½ cup (125 mL) grated Parmesan cheese

Cook lasagna noodles until tender and drain and rinse under cold water. Set aside. In boiling salted water, poach raw seafood until barely cooked. Drain and reserve. Briefly blanch spinach, drain well and chop. Lightly beat eggs. In a large bowl, combine eggs, spinach and cottage cheese. Season with salt, pepper and nutmeg. Set aside.

Preheat oven to 350°F (180°C). Melt butter and sauté onion and garlic until soft. Add dill, flour, salt and pepper and cook, stirring constantly, over medium heat for 1 minute. Whisk sherry and cream into flour mixture a little at a time, until smooth and well blended. Cook, stirring constantly, until thickened. Add Swiss cheese and seafood to sauce, stirring until cheese is melted.

To assemble, place half of the noodles in a greased 9" x 13" (22 cm x 33 cm) lasagna pan. Spread half of the spinach mixture over noodles and cover with half of the seafood sauce. Repeat layers and top with grated Parmesan cheese. Bake for 45 minutes to an hour, or until bubbly and lightly browned. Remove from oven and let stand for 10-15 minutes before serving.

Serves 6-8.

Lobster in Bengali Sauce with Mango Rice

Old House Restaurant, Courtenay, BC

The chili peppers determine the amount of "heat" in this dish. If a milder sauce is to your liking, use 1 pepper or 1 tsp (5 mL) minced jalapeño pepper (seeds and white membrane removed).

few drops sesame oil
2 tsp (10 mL) vegetable oil
1 medium onion, diced
3 garlic cloves, finely minced
2 tsp (10 mL) grated fresh ginger
2 mild chili peppers, seeded and finely diced
   (Ancho, Anaheim, Poblano, etc.)
2 cups (500 mL) coconut milk
1 tsp (5 mL) ground coriander
1 tsp (5 mL) turmeric
pinch of cinnamon
1 tsp (5 mL) curry powder
1½ lb (650 g) cooked lobster, in bite-sized
   chunks
2 tomatoes, diced
salt and pepper
mango rice (recipe follows)

Heat sesame oil and vegetable oil over medium heat in a deep frying pan. Sauté onion for 3 minutes, stirring frequently. Add garlic, fresh ginger, diced tomatoes and chili peppers and continue to cook for 1 minute. Add coconut milk, coriander, turmeric, cinnamon and curry powder and simmer for 10 minutes. Add cooked lobster and diced tomatoes. Cover and let simmer for 2-3 minutes. Adjust seasoning with salt and pepper and serve over mango rice.

Serves 6.

Mango Rice
1½ cups (375 mL) long grain rice
3 cups (750 mL) chicken stock
3 tbsp (45 mL) butter
1 ripe mango, peeled and diced
½ each red and green bell peppers
1 stalk lemongrass (white part only), peeled and
   diced
½ cup (125 mL) unsweetened coconut
pinch each of cumin, cardamom, black pepper,
   salt, ginger, turmeric and curry powder

Cook rice in chicken stock according to directions on package. While rice is cooking, melt butter in a skillet and sauté remaining ingredients until peppers are crisp-tender, about 4 minutes. Stir into cooked rice.

Code di Aragosta Alla Suprema (Lobster Tails Supreme)

Da Maurizio, Halifax, NS

If you cannot purchase individual lobster tails, it will be necessary to cook four lobsters weighing 1½ lb (650 g) each, in order to have tails weighing 4-5 oz (125-150 g).

½ cup (125 mL) butter, softened
3 garlic cloves, crushed
3 tbsp (45 mL) parsley, chopped
4 cooked lobster tails, shelled and halved
½ cup (125 mL) white wine
salt and pepper to taste
1 cup (250 mL) heavy cream (35% M.F.)

Blend together butter, garlic and parsley until smooth.

In a skillet over medium-high heat, melt garlic butter. Add lobster tails and sauté for 3 minutes, being careful not to brown butter. Remove lobster with a slotted spoon and reserve. Deglaze pan with wine, season with salt and pepper and reduce liquid by one-half. Add cream and cook until the sauce is thickened. Return lobster to sauce and heat through. Serve immediately with seasonal vegetables of choice.

Serves 4.

Lobster and Scallops with Sun-dried Tomatoes in Basil Cream

Duncreigan Country Inn, Mabou, NS

Sun-dried tomatoes are available either dry or oil-packed. If using the dry variety, reconstitute in warm water to soften, then drain. Always drain tomatoes that are packed in oil.

¾ lb (375 g) large scallops
4 tbsp (60 mL) butter
3-4 shallots, minced
4 cooked lobster tails, split
½ cup (125 mL) white wine
½ cup (125 mL) sun-dried tomatoes,
    reconstituted (or well-drained, seeded,
    chopped tomatoes)
4 tbsp (60 mL) fresh basil, chopped
salt and pepper to taste
dash of cayenne
½ cup (125 mL) heavy cream (35% M.F.)
4 oz (125 g) Havarti cheese, grated
fresh pasta to serve 4

Sauté scallops in butter over medium-high heat for 1 minute. Add shallots and lobster tails. Bring to a simmer and cook only until scallops are opaque, about 2 more minutes. Remove from pan and keep warm. Deglaze pan with wine; add tomatoes and basil. Season with salt, pepper and cayenne. Add cream and simmer sauce to thicken slightly. Stir in cheese and heat until melted. Return seafood to sauce and serve immediately over prepared pasta.

Serves 4.

East Coast Mornay Sauce

Vineland Estates Winery Restaurant, Vineland, ON

Ever wonder what to do with the body and legs of your steamed lobster? In this recipe, the chef of Vineland Estates Winery Restaurant shares his secrets, telling us how to make this succulent sauce to serve over white fish or crèpes, or as a dipping sauce. For the photo, we served grilled haddock napped with the sauce.

bodies, legs, and shells of 2-3 lobsters
3 cups (750 mL) heavy cream (35% M.F.)
juice of ½ lemon
1 bay leaf
2 tbsp (30 mL) tomato paste
salt and white pepper
grated Parmesan cheese

Prepare lobster carcasses by reserving any tomalley or roe and discarding stomach, eyes and digestive tract. Crush shells and bodies and place in a heavy saucepan with tomalley, roe, cream, lemon juice and bay leaf. Bring to simmer and cook gently for 50 minutes, stirring occasionally with a wooden spoon. Place a small amount of cream mixture in a bowl and stir in tomato paste. Return to saucepan and simmer for 10 minutes longer.

Strain mixture through a fine sieve, being sure to extract all the juices and tiny bits of lobster meat. Return to a clean saucepan and bring to serving temperature. Adjust seasoning with salt and pepper. Stir in Parmesan cheese, 1 tbsp (15 mL) at a time, until sauce reaches desired thickness.

Yields 1½ cups (375 mL).

Index

a

Acton's Grill and Café, Wolfville, NS 58
All Seasons Café, Nelson, BC 38
Amherst Shore Country Inn, Lorneville, NS 84
Astice con Funghi (Lobster with Wild Mushrooms) 74
Atlantic Blue Mussel Chowder 36
Atlantic Crab Dip, Hot 16

b

Barbecued Lobster with Red Pepper and Lime Butter 68
Basil Purée 71
Béarnaise Sauce 19
Bisque, Lobster 42
Black Olive Couscous 71
Blomidon Inn, Wolfville, NS 63
Blue Cheese Sauce, Mussels in 64
Boffins Club, Saskatoon, SK 22
Broiled Mussels 17
Broth, Tomato Olive 71

c

C Restaurant, Vancouver, BC 24, 42
Cappesante di Chioggra (Scallops Chioggra Style) 78
Catch Restaurant, Calgary, AB 29
Chicken and Lobster Supreme 81
chowders
    Atlantic Blue Mussel 36
    Creamy Clam 35
    Lobster 40
    Seafood with Lobster 32
    Clam Chowder, Creamy 35
Clams, Steamed 24
Club Sandwich, Lobster 49
Code di Aragosta Alla Suprema (Lobster Tails Supreme) 89
Coleslaw, Jamaican 69
Compass Rose, Grand Manan Island, NB 51, 86
Coquille St. Jacques 83
Couscous, Black Olive 71
Cozze al Forno (Broiled Mussels) 17
Crab Cakes, Cream Cheese 22
Crab Crêpes with Lemon Caper Sauce 56
Crab Dip, Hot 16
Crab Noodle Soup, Thai 38
Crab Salad 28

Crab-stuffed Tomatoes 20
Cream Cheese Crab Cakes 22
Cream Sauce 47
Creamy Clam Chowder 35
Creole Mustard Sauce 23
Crêpes, Crab with Lemon Caper Sauce 56

d

Da Maurizio, Halifax, NS 74, 89
Dalvay by the Sea, Dalvay, PEI 68
Dip, Hot Crab 16
Diva at the Met, Vancouver, BC 76
Dufferin Inn and San Martello Dining Room, Saint John, NB 52
Duncreigan Country Inn, Mabou, NS 90
Dunes Café (The), Brackley Beach, PEI 32
Dunes' Seafood Chowder with Lobster 32
Dungeness Crab Salad 28
Dungeness Crab-stuffed Heirloom Tomatoes 20

e

East Coast Mornay Sauce 93
Edgewater Manor Restaurant, Stoney Creek, ON 65

f

Fish Stock 32
Fresh Atlantic Lobster Soufflé 58
Fresh Steamed Lobster Compass Rose 73

g

Gazpacho with Shrimp 34
Gnocchi 76
Gremolata 47

h

Haddon Hall Inn, Chester, NS 34
Hot Atlantic Crab Dip 16
Huron County Lobster Chowder 40

i

Inn at Bay Fortune (The), Bay Fortune, PEI 71
Inn on the Cove and Spa, Saint John, NB 82
Inn on the Lake, Waverley, NS 54
Innlet Café, Mahone Bay, NS 48

j

Jamaican Coleslaw 69

l

La Perla, Dartmouth, NS 17, 78
Lake Louise Station, Lake Louise, AB 25
Lasagna, Seafood 86
Le Gavroche, Vancouver, BC 28
Lemon Caper Sauce 57
Lemon Steamed Mussels 48
Linguini, Lobster 63
Little Inn of Bayfield, Bayfield, ON 40
Lobster and Chicken Supreme 81
Lobster and Pasta 60
Lobster and Scallops with Sun-dried Tomatoes in Basil
    Cream 90
Lobster Bisque 42
Lobster Chowder 40
Lobster Club Sandwich 49
Lobster Emulsion 77
Lobster in Bengali Sauce with Mango Rice 88
Lobster in Vanilla Cream Sauce 65
Lobster Linguini 63
Lobster Newburg 84
Lobster on Potato Pancakes with Sour Cream Sauce 52
Lobster Oriental 82
Lobster Potato Salad 29
Lobster Ravioli in Lemon Cream 46
Lobster Rolls 51
Lobster Soufflé 58
Lobster Tails Supreme 89
Lobster Toast Points 54
Lobster Truffle Gnocchi with Lobster Emulsion 76
Lobster with Wild Mushrooms 74
Lobster, Barbecued, with Red Pepper and Lime Butter 68
Lobster, Steamed 73
Lobster-stuffed Mushroom Caps 19

m

Maestro SVP, Montreal, QC 64
Mango Rice 88
Marshlands Inn, Sackville, NB 81
Mediterranean Seafood Stew 36
Mornay Sauce 93
Mountain Gap Inn, Smiths Cove, NS 51
Mushroom Caps, Lobster-stuffed 19
Mushrooms, Wild, with Lobster 74
Mussel Chowder 36
Mussels in Blue Cheese Sauce 64
Mussels, Broiled 17
Mussels, Lemon Steamed 48
Mustard Sauce, Creole 23

n

Nemo's Restaurant, Halifax, NS 37
Newburg, Lobster 84

o

Off Broadway Café, Charlottetown, PEI 19
Old House Restaurant, Courtenay, BC 26, 88
Olive Couscous 71
Oriental Lobster 82

p

Pan-seared Scallops with Black Olive Couscous, Basil
    Purée and Tomato Olive Broth 71
pasta
    Lobster Linguini 63
    Lobster Ravioli in Lemon Cream 46
    Quaco Inn Lobster and Pasta 60
Pepper Sauce 20
Potato Pancakes with Lobster and Sour Cream Sauce
    52
Potato Salad, with Lobster 29

q

Quaco Inn, St. Martins, NB 60
Quaco Inn Lobster and Pasta 60

r

Raincity Grill, Vancouver, BC 20
Ravioli, Lobster in Lemon Cream 46
Red Pepper and Lime Butter 68
Rice, Mango 88
Roasted Roma Tomatoes with Scallops 25
Roll, Lobster 51

s

salads
Crab Salad 28
    Jamaican Coleslaw 69
    Lobster Potato Salad 29
    Sandwich, Lobster Club 49
sauces
    Basil Cream 90
    Bengali Sauce 88
    Blue Cheese Sauce 64
    Cream Sauce 47
    Creole Mustard Sauce 23
    Lemon Caper Sauce 57
    Lobster Emulsion 76

Mornay Sauce 93
Red Pepper and Lime Butter 68
Sour Cream Sauce 52
Tomato Olive Broth 71
Trio of Pepper Sauce 20
Vanilla Cream Sauce 65
scallops
   Chioggra Style Scallops 78
   Coquille St. Jacques 83
   Lobster and Scallops with Sun-dried Tomatoes 90
   Pan-seared Scallops 71
   Scallops with Roasted Roma Tomatoes 25
Seafood Chowder with Lobster 32
Seafood Lasagna 86
Seafood Stew, Mediterranean 37
Shaw's Hotel, Brackley Beach, PEI 35
Shellfish with Yucatan Flavours 26
Shrimp, Gazpacho with 34
Simply Steamed Clams 24
Soufflé, Lobster 58
Sour Cream Sauce 52
Steamed Lobster 73
Steamed Mussels, Lemon 48

Step'n Out Eclectic Cuisine, Winnipeg, MB 46
Stew, Mediterranean Seafood 37
Stock for lobster 74
Stock, Fish 32
Stories Restaurant at Halliburton House Inn, Halifax, NS 83
Sun-dried Tomatoes, with Lobster and Scallops in Basil Cream 90
Supreme, Lobster and Chicken 81
Supreme, Lobster Tails 89

t
Thai Crab Noodle Soup 38
Tomato Olive Broth 71
Tomatoes, Crab-stuffed 20
Tomatoes, Roasted Roma with Scallops 25
Trio of Pepper Sauce 20

v
Vanilla Cream Sauce 65
Vineland Estates Winery Restaurant, Vineland, ON 93

Photo Credits

Cover: Steven Isleifson (back centre); all other photos by Janet Kimber

Hamid Attie: pages 42, 88; Clearwater Seafoods: pages 4, 8 (bottom), 9; Formac Publishing: (Meghan Collins: pages 1, 3, 5, 14-15, 18, 25, 26, 27, 35, 37, 44-45, 48, 54, 57, 60, 63, 69, 72, 75, 77, 87, 96; Elizabeth Eve: page 6; Robert MacGregor: pages 11, 16, 64); Steven Isleifson: pages 30-31, 33, 34, 49, 50, 53, 55, 59, 61, 62, 66, 67, 70, 78-79, 80, 82, 83, 85, 91, 92; Janet Kimber: pages 17, 21, 23, 24, 28, 29, 36, 39, 41, 43, 47, 56, 65, 89; Eliza Manuel: pages 7 (top), 13 (bottom); Nova Scotia Fisheries and Agriculture: page 12; Keith Vaughan: pages 7 (bottom), 8 (top), 10, 13 (top)

Food styling by James MacDougall